I0801720

The INSIDE GUIDE

CELEBRATING HISPANIC CULTURES

Celebrating the People of Costa Rica

By Rosie Banks

Cavendish Square
New York

Published in 2023 by Cavendish Square Publishing, LLC
29 E. 21st Street New York, NY 10010

Website: cavendishsq.com

Library of Congress Cataloging-in-Publication Data

Names: Banks, Rosie, 1978- author.
Title: Celebrating the people of Costa Rica / Rosie Banks.
Description: New York : Cavendish Square Publishing, [2023] | Series: The inside guide: celebrating Hispanic cultures | Includes index.
Identifiers: LCCN 2021037970 (print) | LCCN 2021037971 (ebook) | ISBN 9781502664501 (library binding) | ISBN 9781502664488 (paperback) | ISBN 9781502664495 (set) | ISBN 9781502664518 (ebook)
Subjects: LCSH: Costa Rica–Juvenile literature. | Costa Rica–Social life and customs–Juvenile literature.
Classification: LCC F1543.2 .B36 2023 (print) | LCC F1543.2 (ebook) | DDC 972.86–dc23
LC record available at https://lccn.loc.gov/2021037970
LC ebook record available at https://lccn.loc.gov/2021037971

Editor: Therese Shea
Copyeditor: Jill Keppeler
Designer: Deanna Paternostro

The photographs in this book are used by permission and through the courtesy of: Cover SALMONNEGRO-STOCK/Shutterstock.com; pp. 4, 14-15 (bottom) Luis Alvarado Alvarado/Shutterstock.com; pp. 6-7 Joshua ten Brink/Shutterstock.com; pp. 8-9 Cris Young/Shutterstock.com; p. 10 Joan Arturo/Shutterstock.com; pp. 12-13 Gianfranco Vivi/Shutterstock.com; p. 14 Dmitry Burlakov/Shutterstock.com; p. 16 Raquel Rovira/Shutterstock.com; p. 18 Cara Koch/Shutterstock.com; p. 20 EQRoy/Shutterstrock.com; p. 21 Kevin Valverde Salazar/Shutterstock.com; p. 22 Inspired By Maps/Shutterstock.com; pp. 22-23 (bottom) ESTELLE R/Shutterstock.com; pp. 24-25 Sara Valenti/Shutterstock.com; p. 26 lev radin/Shutterstock.com; p. 27 Wollertz/Shutterstock.com; p. 28 (flag) Steve Allen/Shutterstock.com; p. 28 (map) Andrei Minsk/Shutterstock.com; p. 29 (left) Tati Nova photo Mexico/Shutterstock.com; p. 29 (center) Allison Hays - Allicat Photography/Shutterstock.com; p. 29 (right) Serge Goujon/Shutterstock.com.

CPSIA compliance information: Batch #CS23CSQ: For further information contact Cavendish Square Publishing LLC, New York, New York, at 1-877-980-4450.

Printed in the United States of America

CONTENTS

As of 2021, there were more than 5 million people living in Costa Rica. About half live in cities.

THE HISPANIC HERITAGE OF COSTA RICA

Chapter One

The word "Hispanic" is related to language. It describes people who are from (or whose **ancestors** were from) countries where Spanish is the main language. There are more than 20 such countries around the world. However, Hispanic people don't think of themselves as just one group, and there is no single Hispanic culture or identity. In fact, language may seem like the only thing two Hispanic people have in common.

Many people in the United States choose to identify themselves with their family's country or area of origin. As of 2018, more than 154,000 people in the United States report that Costa Rica is their country of origin. This Hispanic country has a **unique** culture of rich traditions.

About Costa Rica

Costa Rica, a Central American nation, is bordered by the countries of Nicaragua to the north and Panama to the south. It has large bodies of water on both sides. The Pacific Ocean is on Costa Rica's western coast, and the Caribbean Sea is on its eastern coast.

Fast Fact

The number of Spanish speakers in the United States, including those from Costa Rica, makes it the second largest Spanish-speaking country in the world.

WORDS ARE IMPORTANT

You may have heard someone use the term "Hispanic" to describe people when they actually should say "Latino." These two terms are often confused. "Latino," "Latina," and the **gender-neutral** term "Latinx" describe a person living in the United States whose ancestors are from Latin America, including the Portuguese-speaking country of Brazil. Some people don't use any of these terms to describe themselves. When someone tells you how to talk about their identity, it's important to honor that by using the exact language they prefer. Don't be afraid to ask them. That's a sign of respect and will be appreciated.

Fast Fact

About 75 percent of Costa Rica's land is covered in forests. This makes the country a popular place for scientists to research plants and wildlife.

Two mountain ranges run nearly the entire length of Costa Rica. There are active volcanoes in these mountains, including two of the highest peaks: Irazú and Poás. More than half of Costa Ricans live in the Valle Central ("Central Valley"), the highland valley in the center of the country.

Costa Rica has only about 0.03 percent of the world's landmass, but it's thought to contain nearly 5 percent of Earth's plant and animal species.

Parts of Costa Rica receive a lot of rain. The rainiest month, September, can bring more than 12 inches (30 centimeters) of rain. Temperatures vary throughout the country, but it's generally warm, averaging about 70 degrees Fahrenheit (21 degrees Celsius) in San José, the country's capital.

Languages

One of the interesting things about language is that even if people are speaking the same one, it can sound different depending on where they live. For example, the Spanish spoken in Spain sounds much different than the Spanish spoken in Costa Rica. In Spanish, if you want to say something is small, it's common to add "-ito" to the end of a word. Costa Ricans and others, such as Venezuelans and Cubans, use "-ico" instead. That's why Costa Ricans are sometimes nicknamed "Ticos."

Spanish explorers brought their Spanish language with them when they arrived in Costa Rica. Spanish has been spoken there ever since, and today, it's the official language. However, Bribrí, Cabécar, Maléku Jaíka, Boruca, and Térraba are native languages spoken in Costa Rica. Today, less than 1 percent of Costa Rica's population is **indigenous**, but the country's history begins with their ancestors.

Fast Fact

In Costa Rica, women are called Ticas, while men are Ticos. However, the population as a whole is called Ticos as well.

According to the last census, or official count, in 2011, there are around 104,000 indigenous people in Costa Rica.

Many indigenous people in Costa Rica today, such as the Cabécar, still live in the mountains. For some, this means they are cut off from the rest of society.

HISTORY THROUGH TODAY

Chapter Two

Perhaps as many as 400,000 indigenous people lived in the area now called Costa Rica before Europeans came in the 16th century. The Chorotega were among the most powerful when the Spanish arrived.

Christopher Columbus sailed to Costa Rica in 1502, and the first permanent Spanish settlement, the village of Cartago in the Valle Central, was established in 1564. The Spanish didn't spend much time developing Costa Rica or trying to **conquer** it. To them, the lands didn't seem to have riches to claim or a large population to conquer like other Central and South American countries had.

After the Spanish arrived, the indigenous population declined significantly. Slavery and war with the Spanish were two reasons. Europeans also spread deadly diseases to the native peoples that they had never experienced before. Many of the indigenous peoples who did survive moved into the mountains to avoid Spanish rule.

> **Fast Fact**
>
> *Costa Rica* means "rich coast" in Spanish. Some say Christopher Columbus called it that first, but others think this is just a story.

A Democracy

Costa Rica stands apart from many of its neighboring countries because

San José is both the capital and largest city in Costa Rica. It's a center of the nation's culture.

it's a more politically stable country. Along with other Latin American countries, Costa Rica declared independence from Spain in 1821. Its early **progressive** government invested in coffee, bananas, and railroads, which helped make the country strong enough to support itself. Today, Costa Rica is a

democratic republic. Citizens over the age of 18 can vote in elections every four years, much like in the United States.

The Costa Rican constitution makes education free for everyone. The government invests a lot in education—almost a fourth of its budget. Ninety-five percent of Costa Rica's adult population can read and write, and its national university is one of the best in Central America.

Fast Fact

Ecotourism—tourism directed at and in support of nature—is a major source of income for Costa Rica. The beautiful landscapes offer visitors activities such as hiking, surfing, and zip-lining through the Costa Rican rain forests.

The Population Today

About 80 percent of Costa Rica's population today is of European and mestizo **descent**. "Mestizo" means a person has European and indigenous ancestry. A small number of people have a blend of European, indigenous, and African ancestry. Some Costa Ricans are of Chinese descent; an even smaller number of Costa Ricans are of African descent alone. A very small percentage of Costa Ricans are of indigenous ancestry alone. Hundreds of thousands of people have **immigrated** to Costa Rica from

Costa Rica has one of the world's lowest migration rates, which means not many people move away.

DISCRIMINATION

Many Costa Ricans with African ancestors are descendants of enslaved Africans and Black workers who came from the West Indies in the 19th century to build the country's railroads and work on large farms called plantations. Black Costa Ricans were **discriminated** against through laws that limited the places where they could live and travel within the country. They couldn't become citizens either. There were even laws that said plantation owners couldn't hire Black people to work for them. While these laws were **abolished** in 1949, discrimination still exists in Costa Rica, which makes it hard for the Black community to experience full equality.

Fast Fact

Tens of thousands of people in Costa Rica are retired Americans.

the neighboring country of Nicaragua and other Central American countries, sometimes because of economic and political troubles in those nations.

Most Costa Ricans in the Valle Central are of Spanish ancestry. Many people from the smaller populations are scattered around Costa Rica's coasts, highlands, and plains.

The city of Barva, north of San José, is known for its talented mask makers. Since 2002, the National Day of the Costa Rican **Masquerade** has been celebrated in Barva with parades and music.

HOLIDAYS AND OTHER TRADITIONS

Chapter Three

Costa Ricans observe many holidays and festivals throughout the year. Many people are Roman Catholic, so the country honors several Catholic religious holidays and holy days. One of the most important of these occasions is called Semana Santa, or Holy Week. Whole cities and towns shut down during these days, which lead up to the celebration of Easter. Buses stop running, businesses close, and many people attend processions, church services, and other events.

Every year during January, Costa Ricans celebrate the Fiestas Palmares. Called the country's "biggest cowboy party," it's a two-week festival of music, bullfighting, parades, dancing, **rodeos**, and more. It's such a popular event that close to a million people attend it annually.

Fast Fact

Costa Ricans often go to the country's national beaches on holidays.

Clothing

While Costa Ricans often dress in Western-style clothing, like much of the clothing you see in your community, you might see traditional clothing during certain festivals. Those who perform folk dances often wear traditional clothes, for example. Men may wear a wide-brim hat, a

These women are dancing in traditional Costa Rican clothes during a parade.

DÍA DE JUAN SANTAMARÍA

Día de Juan Santamaría (Juan Santamaría Day) is celebrated across Costa Rica on April 11. Juan Santamaría is one of the country's national heroes. According to legend, Santamaría, though just a teenager, was responsible for the Costa Rican victory in the Battle of Rivas in 1856 against William Walker of the United States and his army. Walker was trying to overthrow the Costa Rican government and build a slave-trade empire in Central America. Santamaría volunteered to set fire to a fort where Walker and his troops were staying in Nicaragua. The enemy army was driven out, but Santamaría was killed too. His courage is remembered with parades and ceremonies.

Fast Fact

The seven provinces of Costa Rica are Alajuela, Cartago, Guanacaste, Heredia, Limón, Puntarenas, and San José.

white shirt with a bright red belt, and a red handkerchief with a knot tied in the front. Women may wear a long, layered skirt and a ruffled white top with trim that matches their skirt.

However, each of the seven provinces of Costa Rica has its own unique traditional clothing. For example, in the province of Alajuela, a woman may wear a black ribbon around her neck with a gold cross hanging from it. Men there may wear blue jeans instead of light-colored pants.

Foods

The festivals and holidays of Costa Rica usually involve food—and lots of it! Shrimp and rice is a Semana Santa dish. The traditional Christmas dish is tamales, which are often made with beans and a kind of dough made from corn and are wrapped in banana leaves. Tamales can also include rice and meat such as beef, chicken, or pork.

Rice, beans, and corn play a big part in everyday Costa Rican cooking too. Casado and gallo pinto are two popular Costa Rican dishes.

A plantain is laid over the top of this traditional Costa Rican meal called casado.

Fast Fact

The arabica coffee plant was first grown in Costa Rica in the 1700s. Costa Rica is the world's 13th largest coffee producer.

coffee harvesting

Casado is a meal with beans, rice, vegetables, tortillas, and meat served side by side. *Gallo pinto* means "spotted rooster" in Spanish. Gallo pinto is a dish of rice and beans that are mixed together, giving it a spotted appearance.

Another major Costa Rican food product that's enjoyed around the world is coffee. It's found in every restaurant. However, bananas and pineapples—not coffee—are the top two Costa Rican food exports today.

In archaeology, man-made stone spheres are called petrospheres. More than 300 are found in Costa Rica.

Chapter Four

THE ARTS

Costa Ricans share a love for the arts. Films, live theater, music, and television are popular interests among those who live there.

The country's National Symphony Orchestra, also called the OSN, gave its first concert in 1971. It's hailed as one of the best orchestras, or large classical music groups, in Latin America and has won Grammy Awards in the United States for its recordings.

Famous Costa Rican authors include Fabián Dobles, Carlos Luis Fallas, and Carmen Naranjo. Often, the works of Costa Rican writers focus on the daily lives of the people.

Costa Rica's indigenous and folk art is highly prized. Large stone statues and spheres of carved stone have been found around the country. The stone spheres are believed to have decorated the houses of indigenous leaders, but their exact purpose is unknown. Figurines made of gold and jade are treasured too. Costa Rican folk art is famous for its colorful, highly decorated wooden carvings and carts.

Fast Fact

Built in 1897, the National Theatre in San José is one of the most beautiful structures in Costa Rica. Today, Costa Ricans and visitors attend the National Theatre to see musical performances and live theater.

Music

Guanacaste, the northwest province of Costa Rica, is home to Costa Rica's most well-known folk music traditions. Folk music is traditional music of an area that has been passed down over generations. Costa Rican folk music sometimes features the ocarina and the marimba.

The marimba is so important that the government made November 30 the National Day of the Costa Rican Marimba.

An ocarina is a wind instrument that's often shaped somewhat like a potato. It has a mouthpiece and small finger holes used to make different notes. The Costa Rican ocarina, called a dru mugata, is different from most ocarinas because it's made of beeswax.

The marimba is a percussion instrument. The player hits wooden keys with large mallets to produce notes. Three or more people at a time may play a large marimba. It can create beautiful music for dancing.

Dancing

Dance halls and dance clubs, called discotheques, are popular in San José. On weekends, the clubs are full of Ticos hoping to dance the night away. Dance halls play everything from today's popular music to traditional Latin music such as salsa, merengue, and bachata.

Folk dancing is a way for Costa Ricans to celebrate their **heritage**. As it is for folk music, Guanacaste is the heart of traditional Costa Rican dancing. A performance is a must-see for tourists. While musicians keep time with guitars, a dru mugata, and marimbas, dancers in traditional costumes perform with style. Women spin in their large skirts and wave scarves, relating stories of love to their audience.

Fast Fact

Costa Ricans enjoy many kinds of music, including classical, rock, and American pop music. The country has many radio stations.

COSTA RICAN FÚTBOL

Sports are another large part of many countries' cultures. The most popular sport in Costa Rica by far is football, or *fútbol*, which is called soccer in the United States. There are dozens of football clubs and regional teams throughout the small country today. Nicknamed Los Ticos, Costa Rica's national team (*shown below*) is the most successful of all the Central American teams, making five World Cup appearances as of 2021. Other popular sports in Costa Rica include bullfighting, surfing, volleyball, golf, and fishing.

In Costa Rica, children are taught many of the traditional dances at a young age.

Fast Fact

In the traditional dance called the El Torito ("Little Bull"), one partner, usually the man, plays a dancing bull and the other, usually the woman, dances as a bullfighter staying gracefully away.

Costa Rican culture continues to change and grow with its people. Embracing new traditions and celebrating old ones are both ways to keep the Costa Rican cultural identity meaningful and vibrant.

NEED-TO-KNOW INFO

Kind of Government

democratic republic

Population

5,151,140 (estimate, 2021)

Total Area

19,730 square miles (51,100 square kilometers)

Capital City

San José

Official Country Name

Republic of Costa Rica (República de Costa Rica)

Kind of Money

colon (colones)

Highest Point

Cerro Chirripó—12,530 feet (3,819 meters)

Flag

Location

THINK ABOUT IT!

1. Why might people not use the terms "Hispanic" or "Latino" to describe themselves even though they're from a country with Spanish-speaking people?
2. Why do you think each province of Costa Rica has traditional clothing that's a bit different from the others?
3. Think of a cultural tradition from your background that is similar to one you read about in this book. How are they alike?
4. Do you think it's important for people to keep their traditions when they move to a new country? Why or why not?

GLOSSARY

abolish: To officially end or stop something.

ancestor: Someone who comes before others in their family tree.

conquer: To take over.

democratic republic: A form of government in which voting citizens elect representatives who run the government on their behalf.

descent: The background of a person in terms of their family or nationality.

discriminate: To treat people unequally based on class, race, religion, or another factor.

gender-neutral: Not referring specifically to a certain gender.

heritage: The traditions or beliefs that are part of the history of a group or nation.

immigrate: To come to a country to live there.

indigenous: Having to do with the first people of an area.

masquerade: A celebration in which masks and costumes are worn.

progressive: Interested in or using new or modern ideas.

rodeo: A contest of many events involving cowboy skills.

unique: Being the only one of its kind.

FIND OUT MORE

Books

Anderson, Corey. *Costa Rica*. Minneapolis, MN: Bearport Publishing, 2020.

Klepeis, Alicia. *Costa Rica*. Minneapolis, MN: Bellwether Media, 2020.

Kopp, Megan. *Costa Rica*. New York, NY: AV2 by Weigl, 2018.

Websites

Costa Rica
kids.nationalgeographic.com/geography/countries/article/costa-rica
National Geographic Kids has more facts about the country's wildlife.

Costa Rica for Kids
www.kids-world-travel-guide.com/costa-rica-facts.html
Learn more facts about the Central American nation here.

Costa Rica Tourism Board
www.visitcostarica.com/en
This is the official site for travelers to Costa Rica.

INDEX